War in the Gulf

GEORGE BUSH

Written By: Paul J. Deegan

Published by Abdo & Daughters, 6535 Cecilia Circle, Edina, Minnesota 55439.

Library bound edition distributed by Rockbottom Books, Pentagon Tower, P.O. Box 36036, Minneapolis, Minnesota 55435.

Library of Congress Number: 91-073077   ISBN: 1-56239-024-4

Cover Photo by: UPI Bettmann
Inside Photos by: UPI Bettmann
                   Wideworld Photos: 20

Edited by: Rosemary Wallner

TABLE OF CONTENTS

GULF VICTORY — A GREAT TRIUMPH

"Kuwait is liberated."

"Iraq's army is defeated."

President George Bush making a serious appeal to Saddam Hussein to get out of Kuwait.

Those were the first words spoken by George Bush when he addressed the nation on February 27, 1991. Speaking from the Oval Office in the White House, he was announcing that the fighting would end in Operation Desert Storm. It had been, he said, a "quick, decisive, and just" victory.

The president's solemn, almost stern appearance could not have reflected his inner feelings. For this night marked his greatest triumph in a quarter-century of government service.

The United States, under his direction, had taken on an international bully, and the success of the undertaking was total and complete. The Iraq army fled from Kuwait, which it had invaded on August 2, 1990. The cost in lives to the Americans and their allies in the fighting was unbelievably low. Fewer than 100 American men and women had been killed in the military operation.

"Seven months ago, America and the world drew a line in the sand," President Bush said. "We declared that the aggression against Kuwait would not stand."

"Tonight, " he told the television audience, "Kuwait is once more in the hands of Kuwaitis. (They are) in control of their own destiny."

FAMILY BACKGROUND

George Herbert Walker Bush, the 41st president of the United States, was born June 12, 1924, in Milton, Massachusetts, near Boston. George was the second son of Prescott and Dorothy Walker Bush. Both parents were from wealthy families.

George's mother named him after her father, George Herbert Walker. She called her father "Pop" so young George came to be called "Poppy." The name stuck with him into his college days.

George's parents both came from the Midwest. His father was from Columbus, Ohio; his mother from St. Louis, Missouri. Dorothy's father, G.H. Walker, had worked in the family business after returning from England. His parents had sent him there to study. The family business was Ely Walker & Company. It was "then the largest dry-goods wholesaler west of the Mississippi," George Bush has said. G.H. Walker left the business to begin his own investment firm.

Once a boxer, then a polo player, Walker later became an avid golfer. A close friend of his had begun the international tennis competition known as the Davis Cup. G.H. Walker started a similar competition for golfers in 1923. Amateur golfers from the United States and Great Britain still play for the Walker Cup every year.

George Bush's other grandfather, Samuel P. Bush, was president of a steel casting company in Columbus. In the summer, George's father went to the family resort at Watch Hill, Rhode Island. Prescott Bush returned to the East to go to college. He graduated from Yale and then enlisted in the Army after the United States entered World War I. He served in Europe and came out of the service a captain.

After the war, George's father began a career in business management. He specialized in taking over troubled companies. George has said his father reorganized them, "turning money losers into profit makers." Prescott Bush's career kept the family on the move for a while. George was born in Milton while his father worked for the United States Rubber Company.

The Bush family lived in a large, three-story home in Milton. The house had a huge front porch. But U.S. Rubber soon moved its headquarters to New York City. When George was a year old, the Bush family resettled in Greenwich, Connecticut, a town that had many expensive residential estates.

When George's father was 31, he joined the New York investment banking firm of W.A. Harriman. The major owner, W. Averell Harriman, later held top U.S. government posts. The firm's president was G.H. Walker, Prescott's father-in-law. The Harriman firm later merged with another well-known financial company. The new company was very successful. Prescott Bush began to build his own fortune and became an investor in some major campanies. Among them were Pan American Airways and the Columbia Broadcasting System.

George's father was a large man, 6'4" and some 200 pounds. He had been a championship golfer as a youth. He eventually served as the president of the U.S. Golf Association, as had his father-in-law. Prescott Bush also loved music. He often sang with small and large vocal groups. He was a stern, but loving father, who tolerated no nonsense from his boys. His father, George Bush has said, taught him about "duty and service."

His mother, Bush has recalled, taught him about "dealing with life on a personal basis, relating to other people." Mrs. Bush was, according to her son, "a first-rate athlete." Although a small woman, she was good at sports including tennis and golf.

Religion was a regular part of the family routine. They were Episcopalians. George's parents read Bible lessons to the children at breakfast each day.

GROWING UP

While Prescott Bush's business career flourished, his family grew. After George and his older brother, Prescott Jr., came Nancy. Their brother Jonathan was born in 1931 and William, called "Bucky," followed seven years later. The year Jonathan was born, the family had moved again.

But they stayed in Greenwich. The new home was a two-acre estate. This house had six bedrooms and a very large playroom in the basement. There were rolling lawns and a brook. The Bush family had maids, a cook, and a man who served as handyman, gardener, and sometime-chauffeur.

Mrs. Bush and the children spent summers on the Maine coast at Kennebunkport. Here a peninsula reaching into the Atlantic Ocean was known as Walker's Point. Mrs. Bush's father and grandfather had bought the peninsula in 1899. There were several houses on the 11 acres of property. The Bush family lived in one called "The Bungalow." Prescott Bush would come to Maine for weekends and vacations.

"Maine in the summer was the best of all possible adventures," George Bush wrote years later. George and his older brother slept in a screened-in porch at The Bungalow. Some days they fished from their grandfather's lobster boat, named the *Tomboy*. Their grandfather taught George and Pres how to use the boat. When George was nine years old, he and his brother got the okay to take the *Tomboy* into the Atlantic by themselves for the first time.

President Bush taking some time off from the job and getting some exercise at his summer home in Kennebunkport, Maine.

On that day, no one would have guessed that Kennebunkport, a half-century later, would be the vacation retreat of a United States president. Fifty years later, George Bush continued to enjoy taking a motorboat into the Atlantic. He loves, he has said, "the physical sensation of steering a powerful machine, throttle open in a following sea . . . "

G.H. Walker also owned a plantation in South Carolina. When George was a boy, the family would go there for Christmas.

George Bush's best friend when he was growing up was his older brother Pres. Sister Nancy has said the two "were thick as thieves." They shared activities and companions. They also shared collections of matchboxes, stamps, and baseball cards. The young George Bush was friendly and outgoing. He was always ready to share things with his friends. He also was the best athlete in the family.

"George always was coordinated," Pres has said, "even as a little guy. He had a good pair of eyes, good hands, natural reactions. He caught and hit the (base)ball well. He's always been quick and bright." His brother, he said, was also "a terrible tease."

12

He entered Greenwich Country Day, a private boys school, a year earlier than the norm. Country Day students wore black sweaters with orange stripes. They gathered for prayers each morning. Twice a week the students rode horses at a nearby stable.

When George was 12 years old, he left his Greenwich home to attend an all-boys college preparatory school: Phillips Academy in Andover, Massachusetts. Better known as Andover, the school was founded in 1775. His brother Pres was already there.

By all accounts, George got along well at Andover. In his senior year, however, he developed a bacterial infection in his right arm. Although today's drugs can treat the infection, no such medicine was available then. Bush's parents put him in a Boston hospital and feared that he might die. After several weeks, he recovered. His family decided it would be best for him to stay out of school and regain his strength. He returned to Andover the following fall to begin his senior year once again. That year he was president of the senior class and captain of both the soccer and baseball teams.

BUSH GOES TO WAR

During that final prep school year, the Japanese bombed Pearl Harbor, and the United States entered World War II. Western European nations had already gone to war against Germany and its allies.

Henry Stimson delivered the commencement address at Andover in the spring of 1942. Stimson was the Secretary of War (the position is now called Secretary of Defense). His speech had a powerful impact on the 17-year-old Bush.

The causes and results of this war were a major influence on Bush. His decisions as president to mount Operations Desert Shield and Desert Storm can be related to his experiences in World War II. As president, he had not hesitated to use military force, even before 1990, when he thought vital United States interests were at stake. Earlier, when he was vice president, Bush said in 1983 that the lessons of World War II should never be forgotten. He said then that nations have no choice but to protect themselves "against the bullies who threaten them."

When Bush turned 18 a few weeks after graduating from Andover, he went to Boston and was sworn into the United States Navy. "I'd joined to fly," Bush said in later years. He was the youngest aviator in the Navy when he got his wings. After more flight training, Bush was assigned to a carrier-based torpedo squadron in the Pacific Ocean. He flew a dive-bomber.

On September 2, 1944, on a bombing mission, Bush's plane was hit by Japanese anti-aircraft fire as the plane dove to its target. Though his plane was burning, Bush continued to dive and drop his bombs. He battled to keep the plane aloft for a few miles. He ordered his two crew members to bail out. Then he too parachuted from the damaged plane. He landed in the ocean about 10 miles from the island he had bombed. He had a deep cut on his head from hitting the tail of the plane as he jumped out.

He knew the Japanese would send boats to capture him. He found the seatback rubber raft from his plane and paddled alone in the ocean. Meanwhile, other planes in his squadron attacked the boats sent to find him. After a couple hours alone at sea, Bush saw something nearby on the water. It grew larger until he could see it was a periscope. Soon he saw the rest of the submarine as it surfaced.

Whose submarine was it? It was the U.S. Navy's. They rescued the 20-year-old pilot, but his two crew members perished. For his courage in completing his mission, Bush was awarded the Distinguished Flying Cross.

GEORGE MARRIES AND GOES TO YALE

George Bush came home from the war on Christmas Eve 1944. Two weeks later he married Barbara Pierce in Greenwich. She was from Rye, New York, like Greenwich, a New York City suburban community. Her father was a magazine publisher. George and Barbara had met during a Christmas party in Bush's last year at Andover. They had been secretly engaged in August 1943 when Barbara was 18 years old. They had announced the engagement four months later.

After their marriage, they honeymooned at the Cloisters on Sea Island, Georgia.

George and Barbara first lived in Norfolk, Virginia, where the Navy assigned George to train pilots. The couple was at the officers' club at the Naval Air Station in Norfolk on August 15, 1945, when they heard that the Japanese had surrendered to end World War II. Germany had surrendered on May 7, 1945.

By November 1945, George and Barbara were in New Haven, Connecticut. George had followed his father to Yale University. He majored in economics and earned Phi Beta Kappa honors. He was a fraternity member and was accepted into the prestigious Skull and Bones senior secret society. He played first base on the baseball team. His father also had played baseball at Yale. George was team captain when he was a senior. That year's club made the finals of the National Collegiate Athletic Association tournament. It was the second straight year the team had gone to the College World Series.

THE BUSHES MOVE TO TEXAS

When George graduated from Yale in 1948, he and Barbara were parents of George Walker Bush. The couple and their son, almost two years old, moved to west Texas "to learn the oil business." George decided to go to Texas at the suggestion of a friend of his family, Neil Mallon. Mallon, a Yale graduate, headed Dresser Industries. Prescott Bush was a director of the company. George went to work for a division of Dresser. He started as an equipment clerk and eventually became a salesman.

Less than three years later, Bush set out on his own. With a partner, he became an independent oil producer. The partner was a neighbor in Midland, Texas. Bush had "caught the fever" of the oil business, the partner later recalled. Buying and selling oil leases in west Texas at the time was a way "to make a lot of money quick," Bush had said. An uncle, Herbert Walker, invested nearly half a million dollars in the company.

In 1952 George's father, running as a Republican from Connecticut, was elected to the United States Senate. His father, George has said, "had made his mark in the business world." He entered politics because, "Now he felt he had a debt to pay." Prescott Bush would serve 10 years in the Senate.

Bush's first company merged with another independent oil company in 1953. This company drilled for oil and gas. Within a year, it became very profitable. George then became president of a newly formed division involved with offshore exploration. That company went its own way and moved to Houston, Texas, in 1959. Bush went to Houston to run it.

By this time, the Bush family was complete. John Ellis Bush, called "Zeb," had been born in 1953. Neil Mallon Bush, named after the man who gave George his first job, was born in 1955. Marvin Pierce Bush was born a year later. A daughter, Dorothy Walker Bush, was born in 1959. A first daughter, Robin, had developed leukemia and had died in 1953, two months short of her fourth birthday.

George Bush campaigning for the U.S. Senate with help from his wife, Barbara.

A NEW BUG STRIKES

George had participated in community affairs in Midland. In Houston, he expressed some interest in getting involved in politics. After three years in Houston, he was asked to run for the job of Harris County Republican chairman. It was his first political campaign. His oldest son has described his dad back then as a quiet, modest, even shy man. Yet he was a successful campaigner and was elected chairman.

At the time Houston, as well as the rest of Texas, was a Democratic stronghold. A longtime Bush friend later recalled how it was. "If you were a Texas Republican in the 1950s," he said, "you didn't let anybody know it."

Still, George decided two years later to run for the U.S. Senate. He was then 40 years old. However, his opponent, Ralph Yarborough, a Democrat, was reelected in the 1964 election. Although he lost, George got a higher percentage of the vote than had any previous Republican candidate.

He had also discovered he really liked politics. Earlier, he said he'd been "bitten by the bug" that took him into the oil business. "Now," he said, "I've been bitten by another bug."

Fifteen months later he resigned from his oil company. He had decided to devote all his time to politics.

In 1966, he ran for Congress from a Houston district that included one of the city's most prosperous neighborhoods. He became the first Republican to represent Houston in the House of Representatives.

He arrived in Washington during the Vietnam War. At the time, he supported the war. Later, he favored removing U.S. forces from Southeast Asia. Although President Lyndon Johnson was a Democrat, Bush worked to establish a good relationship with him. Johnson was from the hill country of southwest Texas.

George Bush, first Republican to represent Houston, Texas, in the House of Representatives.

A TRY FOR THE SENATE FAILS

Bush was reelected to Congress in 1968. In that fall's election, Richard Nixon was voted into the White House. Bush made himself known to the new president. Nixon supported Bush when George decided to give up his House seat and again run against Senator Yarborough in 1970.

Helping Bush in the election campaign was a Houston lawyer, James A. Baker III. Bush had met Jim Baker over 10 years earlier. Baker's family had been prominent in Houston since the turn of the century. Bush and Baker became close friends. Both were Ivy League graduates. They lived in a wealthy Houston residential area. Both played tennis at the exclusive Houston Country Club. It was a friendship that later would boost Baker into national prominence.

Their first joint effort was not successful, however, Yarborough didn't make the November election. He was beaten in the Democratic primary by Lloyd Bentsen, a successful businessman and former congressman. Bentsen beat Bush in the general election. The defeat was crushing for Bush. His son, George, said he had never seen his father so far down as after that defeat.

The loss also left Bush without a job. However, President Nixon had an assignment for Bush. The president named him U.S. ambassador to the United Nations. Bush held the post from 1971 until 1973. In New York City, he began to develop the ties with other countries that he would use so skillfully in the Persian Gulf crisis.

It was back to domestic politics in 1973. A reelected President Nixon asked Bush to head the Republican National Committee. It wasn't long before the Watergate scandal occupied the headlines. When Nixon was forced to resign in August 1974, Vice President Gerald Ford became president. Bush hoped he would be named vice president. But it didn't happen.

OFF TO CHINA

Bush thought President Ford might offer him an important diplomatic post abroad. Bush decided he wanted to be the United States envoy in China. At the time, the U.S. did not have formal diplomatic relations with China. Bush asked Ford for the envoy's job. A surprised president gave it to him. George and Barbara lived in Beijing, China, from September 1974 until December of 1975. The Bush children remained in the United States.

As 1976 began, George and Barbara were back in Washington, D.C. President Ford had asked him to run the Central Intelligence Agency (CIA). As CIA director, Bush added to his knowledge of foreign governments. He held the post until Jimmy Carter, a Democrat, defeated Ford in the 1976 presidential election.

President Ford gives Barbara Bush a kiss after George Bush is sworn in as director of the CIA.

"...GEORGE WILL BE PRESIDENT"

Shortly after the 1976 election, CIA chief Bush was in Plains, Georgia, to brief President-elect Carter. A far-range security problem was being discussed. Carter said he wouldn't have to worry about that. "By then George will be president and he can take care of it," Carter said.

Bush had long ago decided he would one day run for president. He now began his quest for the most powerful political position in the free world. But it would not be an easy run. He spent three years campaigning for the 1980 Republican nomination for president. Directing the effort was Jim Baker. However, Ronald Reagan had returned for his second try at becoming the Republican presidential candidate. By the spring of 1980, it was clear Reagan would win the nomination. A disappointed Bush still hoped he might be chosen as Reagan's running mate.

That's what happened in July. In the November election, the former governor of California and Bush crushed the Carter-Walter Mondale team.

George Bush seriously considers the vice-presidency of the United States of America.

It had been a long road. When the Bushes moved into the vice president's home in Washington in January 1981, it was their 28th home. They had lived in 17 cities during their 35 years of marriage. They wouldn't have to move far for the next several years. The Reagan-Bush team overwhelmingly defeated the Democrat's ticket of Mondale and Geraldine Ferraro in 1984.

After a shaky start in Iowa, Bush sailed through the 1988 presidential primary votes. His was the only name presented to the Republican nominating convention. He chose a young Indiana senator, J. Danforth (Dan) Quayle, as his running mate. After the convention, Jim Baker took over as Bush's campaign manager. Baker had resigned as President Reagan's Secretary of the Treasury. Earlier, he had been Reagan's chief of staff.

Running against Bush and Quayle were Democrats Michael Dukakis and Lloyd Bentsen. Dukakis was the third-term governor of Massachusetts. Dukakis' running mate was the same Senator Bentsen who had defeated Bush in the Senate race 18 years earlier. Bush and Quayle won an easy victory on November 8 in an election in which half the eligible voters stayed home.

At age 64, George Bush took the oath of office as the 41st President of the United States on January 20, 1989.

George Bush chooses J. Danforth Quayle as his running mate for the presidential office of the United States.

A LIFETIME IN PREPARATION

A little over 16 months into his term of office, Iraq invaded neighboring Kuwait. President Bush's response was immediate. He had decided to take a stand.

Perhaps as a result of his previous jobs, the president seemed more comfortable with foreign affairs than with domestic problems. Ten years earlier he had said of the presidency, "Domestic problems drag you down and nag all the time.

"But sooner or later something major happens," Bush had said. "Something (happens) abroad that only (the U.S.) can do something about. Then you show if you can cut it."

The crisis in the Middle East was an event "for which Bush has spent a lifetime preparing," one reporter said. It was "the test he knew would come sometime, the challenge he has always been confident he could meet."

And meet it he did.

George Bush built strong relationships with the heads of state throughout his political career.

He began by calling on the contacts he had built up over the past 20 years. The Soviet Union agreed to join a United States blockade of Iraq. The United Nations condemned the takeover of Kuwait and called for Iraq to get out. The president put together a coalition of nearly 30 nations. These countries sent armed forces to the Persian Gulf under Operation Desert Shield. Even Arab nations agreed to provide troops.

Early in the gulf crisis, President Bush had referred back to World War II. "A half century ago, our nation and the world paid dearly for appeasing an aggressor who should, and could, have been stopped." He was referring to Adolf Hitler and his German war machine. "We are not going to make the same mistake again."

The new aggressor who had to be stopped was Iraq's president, Saddam Hussein. To that end, the president had ordered 210,000 U.S. troops to Saudi Arabia on August 7. After the November 1990 elections, he announced that he was doubling the American force in the Gulf. Saddam Hussein placed 500,000 troops in Kuwait and across the border in Southern Iraq.

George Bush calls on Mikhail Gorbachev of the Soviet Union to support the United Nations condemnation over Iraq.

During the troop buildup, the president kept his old friend Jim Baker, busy. Baker, now U.S. Secretary of State, consulted constantly with the Allied Nations. Eventually Baker made a fruitless trip to Geneva, Switzerland. It was a last minute attempt to see if Iraq would accede to the United Nations resolutions and peacefully withdraw from Kuwait.

U.S. Secretary of State James Baker consults with the Allied Nations during Desert Shield troop buildup.

A TOTAL VICTORY

When diplomacy failed, Bush sent his press secretary to announce that under Operation Desert Storm, the "liberation of Kuwait" had begun.

A massive air bombardment of Iraq and Iraqi forces in Kuwait was followed by a ground offensive. The ground war lasted only 100 hours before Bush called it to a halt. Iraq's military machine was virtually destroyed. There had been very few Allied casualties. Coalition forces had retaken Kuwait City, the nation's capital, without a struggle. Operation Desert Storm had taken only six weeks from start to finish. It was a complete and total victory.

President Bush won almost universal praise for his handling of the Persian Gulf conflict. A Washington columnist said, "Bush managed to rally a reluctant nation to a successful war . . . with shrewd and forcing actions." Yet in his February 27 address, he said this was "not time to gloat.

"But," the president added, "it was not time to gloat. But it is a time of pride — pride in our troops, pride in our friends who stood with us during the crisis, pride in our nation . . ."

He spoke of America's "magnificent fighting forces." Then, maintaining the theme he had repeated over and over during the Persian Gulf crisis, he said, " No one country can claim this victory as its own." He said it was "not only a victory for Kuwait, but a victory for all the coalition partners.

"This is a victory for the United Nations, for all mankind, for the rule of law, and for what is right."

No one could have felt prouder than George Bush surely felt that night as he hailed a victory that was "quick, decisive and just."

George and Barbara Bush congratulate the U.S. fighting forces.

THE BUSH FAMILY